KAFKA & I

Can Xue

TRANSLATED BY DEANNA REN

HANUMAN EDITIONS

CONTENTS

vii   Editors' Note

xvii   Prelude

3   Kafka & I

27   Brunelda's Song: Reading Kafka's *Amerika*

51   The Return of Glory: Reading Kafka's 'Josephine the Songstress or The Mouse Folk'

EDITORS' NOTE

Like couplets, strung arm in arm, there are writers who accompany writers, who are followed, observed and mirrored across time. To many, Franz Kafka of twentieth century Prague is one such writer, as the author of stories that line the edges of the real. This volume is concerned with his importance for Can Xue, a celebrated literary figure in modern day China. Can Xue's work is pitched between seen and unseen realms, joining Kafka's lineage as chronicler of the material fantastic, or the mythically irresolute. That is where she locates herself as writer and as reader in this collection of essays for Hanuman, which chart the author's relationship to Kafka through reflections on three episodes in his oeuvre, and in particular, the women who animate it.

EDITOR'S NOTE

Kafka & I opens with an essay of the same name, on Can Xue's discovery of Kafka's novels at an early stage in her life as a young mother. At this key juncture, she began reading Kafka as a harbinger of a "new kind of literature," a literature poised on the border between a quotidian and a more spiritualized existence. Kafka's female artists are conductors of such border spaces, as Can Xue explores in the following two essays, "Brunelda's Song:

Reading Kafka's *Amerika*", and "The Return of Glory—Reading Kafka's 'Josephine the Songstress or The Mouse Folk'". For Brunelda and Josephine, their art is music, but more so music as a site for exchange (indeed, the book's cover evokes Annie Besant and C.W. Leadbeater's thought-form of an opera by Wagner): Brunelda is a "siren", luring the men to her tower for the sake of such conjunction, while Josephine is in service of the miraculous as "window" and muse. The essays model a morphic image of artmaking where spinner, singer, storyteller listens to the celestial and transmits it through the mundane. Yet for Can Xue, such a classically dualistic ideal of artist as conduit must also take on a dimension of multipolar responsibility.

Doubles appear and disappear across the texts. There is, to start with, K. and his castle, Josephine and her audience, Brunelda and her companions, perhaps men and women altogether. A world disappointingly crude and prosaic, offset by aspirations to communicate paradisiacal power. Pain that is contemporary and eternal divides in human nature. Kafka, as echoed by his readers, Can Xue included.

In these essays, it is not only splitting but an active state of self-splitting that she foregrounds as creative practice and literary exercise, all parties striving towards an equilibrium that first lies under a cover of clouds, where meanings are chalky and immense, only to be finally instantiated in a moment of recognition, when binaries dissolve and a "suffering" of silent mirrors, of contradictions between flesh and form, is spoken into grace.

In her prelude, Can Xue calls such a moment, unlikely, albeit narratively commanded, a "most rational cosmic event," a paradigm for artistic realization through which man and woman might "each restore in themselves the essence of the other." This is where Can Xue encounters Kafka, engaging him as an advocate for consciousness, for the integration of fragments of disbanded selfhood, a conversion in which she, and we, are jointly implicated. Can Xue, through this study of Kafka, reimagines our pull towards being as the ideation of that which is, in her words '"Human with a capital H"', human as in whole, synergistically male and female, a union of authorial and receptive conditions, a prioritization of oneness. The writer as he is now, the reader as she continues to become.

PRELUDE

For Kafka, women are the manifestation of yearning, and yearning is the prime mover of art. Seldom is there an author who can write about art as though writing about a woman, and write about women as though writing about art. Women are more finely attuned to their own desires, they yearn beyond imagination to communicate.

In the following two essays on Kafka's women, Brunelda's eruption honestly depicts the original scene of artistic creation as she pushes her strength and her wildest imagination to its limits. And like her, the singer Josephine, too, is an example of a thoroughly manifest woman of desire and artistry. She pursues freedom to its utmost bounds, never satisfied. Yet she is unable to attain any sense of lasting fulfillment from her communicative labors, and instead sinks into eternal torment.

I believe Kafka to be the most feminine-minded of male writers; it is rare for a male writer to immerse himself as deeply in female desire as Kafka does. There is also the fact that I personally see myself as the most masculine minded of female writers. As such, I would say that I am in a unique position to understand Kafka. Such is the mystery of the universe: it would be the most rational cosmic event of all if man and woman were to each restore in themselves the essence of the other. This small volume for Hanuman Editions pays my respect to Kafka's riveting depiction of women.

Can Xue
August 2024

Kafka & I

KAFKA & I

Forty years ago, I was still a housewife and new mother, when, one gloomy day, I happened to begin reading a novel by Kafka. It was this subconscious decision, perhaps, that transformed my entire view of literature, granting in my laborious explorations of it thereafter a conviction in a new kind of literature. What, then, does Kafka mean for a writer of a particular kind of literature like me? Whenever this question is raised, my mind is flooded with scenes of that gloomy afternoon. Utter intoxication of the mind and body; malicious, vengeful delight; a secret, implacable torrent of emotion. Oh, what a demanding exercise of spirit and struggle of bodily willpower that work was. And yet, I felt deeply that its author possessed a beautifully vibrant, crystalline state. It was only because he was simultaneously engaged as angel and demon, well-versed in the art of self-splitting, that he was able to portray this state in a convincing manner.

Years later, I, too, came to pursue such a cause. Only then did I understand that this was a cause most difficult to apprehend; against a backdrop of uncertainty, you could only rely on internal desire and fight desperately to the end. The boundless chaos of the battlefield was like a conspiratorial web, and you a game piece thrown into the fray by chance, forever unable to grasp whether your pursuit was yielding any results. Such is the feeling of a free person, the real freedom transmitted to me by Kafka through the farsighted perspective of his works. It is a kind of freedom that moves one to slough off their mundane outer shell for intrinsic pursuit, a pursuit that wages a contradictory war. So what, then, does Kafka suggest for me? He suggests an incomparably miserable yet impassionedly thrilling freedom, like everything experienced by Josef K in *The Trial*: mystery, horror, unfamiliarity, and through it all, a total adherence to bodily instinct and monumental willpower.

But how to understand K's thrill

as an outsider or onlooker? Was it not precisely for this thrill, for the building of a modern human character, that he resolved to cast off his already corrupted body and modes of thought? And so, even from the very outset, I had not approached this novel as an outsider or onlooker, for this is a literature that transforms one's values, and as such, she will never belong to outsiders or onlookers. "If you come, it will accept you; if you leave, it will let you." The priest's explanation of "the law" in the novel mirrors the author's own state of perception—that of a free person's perception. If we refuse to believe that our stiff limbs are currently marching toward death, if we still want to dance in our chains with imaginative abandon, Kafka's works will imbue us with strength.

This pursuit is a never-ending toil; one must part ways with instinctive inertness, placing themselves before the guillotine to be tried. All one once possessed—dignity, status, thriving self-esteem, even kinship and romantic love—is exposed under that fatally brilliant light to be transformed, and ultimately, shattered into pieces. No one readily accepts this process, so the entirety of life itself becomes an arena of challenge and struggle. So that his reborn body and spirit may rise from these ruins, the muddle-headed surveyor of the castle, K, becomes an athlete in the arena. The hidden castle, shrouded in fog, represents the unfathomable nature of humankind, a contradictory willpower that nevertheless breaks through contradictions and forges ahead.

For K, who experienced the test of death in *The Trial*, the vast, gloomy domain of the castle now looms before his eyes. He resolves to launch an attack on this riddle of human nature that appears before him, striving with an unmatched tenacity and adaptability to achieve a victory of the century.

But what exactly is the mysterious beast he must defeat? To whom does this beast belong? The answers to these questions are extremely ambiguous. A defamiliarized opposite appears in an unyielding stance, restricting one's every move.

Although the protagonist, brimming with untamable energy and imagination, unfailingly suffers defeat in his numerous confrontations with the castle, in him there nonetheless appears the foretelling of a new kind of human character. He possesses an abundance of initiative and explorative zeal, as well as an undaunted spirit, loyal to the end. He is also given to acquiring abstruse knowledge from his opponents, internalizing this learning and transforming it into action.

Amid this rhythm of training and transformation, the initially unfamiliar castle reveals to him, in silence, the rule of a higher state of living. Of course, this rule cannot be wielded as a weapon for his subsequent struggles; it will not grant him any control. It remains that he can only rely on himself, on his fantastical vision, to guide his actions. Even so, having rules and not having them are fundamentally different: rules continually renew one's understanding, expanding the protagonist's horizons, enabling him to eventually see the structure of humanity.

And at last, K comes to personally experience this structure. Feelings of gratitude and resentment between him and the castle encompass the self-restraint of a person in possession of willpower with regards to their bodily impulses. This compulsory self-restraint appears through the image of the castle (sometimes as an official, sometimes as someone else): the manifestation of the protagonist's spirit. Yet the controlled nature of this energy is ambiguous; it often exhibits a striking tendency to flirt with matters of the flesh.

Once a human becomes human, his flesh can never again part

from the spirit's restraint, just as the survival of the spirit can never again part from the eruption of bodily yearning. As the protagonist's exacting mirror, the castle looks past nothing—not his vanity, nor his laziness, nor wishful thinking, or even his attempts to lead a life of indulgence.

What, then, does the castle ask of K? It asks him to "die." But this death does not refer to bodily annihilation, because if the body is annihilated, K cannot produce his spirit. No, the castle's demand for death is rather a demand for the body to experience death, what you might call the spirit's flirtation with the flesh. Given that living is a precondition, all foolish spectacle, humiliation, disdain, deprivation, despairing struggle, shameful defeat, etc., are a matter of course. This messily mundane life of the flesh is precisely what produces a pristine state which becomes the soil of a new, castle-like human character. It is only by the beam of white, somber light from the castle skies that the sordid soil of the mundane realm attains a whole new meaning. This is rich, robust soil, soil from which a hero of an era emerges.

All along, the castle in the fog was self-consciousness, that uniquely human consciousness borne of contradiction between body and spirit. Within this seemingly negatory framing, all human performance is derived only from the eruption of one's inherent core. Mirrors do not speak; mirrors merely perceive down to the finest detail, suspending one in a self-torment given by the hopelessness of the desire to live, and the inability to fulfill the desire to die. This very condition is the womb in which gestates a modern spirit. Thus the story's structure becomes clear: human rationality and the inherent momentum of the flesh; practice and spirit; K and the castle—these are various expressions of the same contradiction.

The hidden castle that K had all this time fought unto death to enter was actually a part of K himself. So long as the body's struggles of the mundane persist, the ideational castle will never disappear. So long as the artist lives, severe self-examination and bold, undaunted efforts of discernment will never cease.

In Western classical philosophy, human nature is split into two components, each contained within its own sphere, unfamiliar with the other. But in any given era, there are always those people in possession of a particularly strong self-consciousness, those who probe into the finer points of human nature to recover the other half, so that they may become "Human" with a capital "H." Artists naturally inclined to sensitivity are among these people. Veiled in a sea of clouds and mountains, their relentlessly progressing cause (just as difficult to describe as the castle and K's internal desires) continues to develop in secret to this day. The people of today—artists included—are those who become deft at self-splitting amid their struggle to survive. Splitting brings us intense pain; its contradictory reality compels us to the extreme state of the artist, and it is here that we meet Kafka.

The bells of a new century are ringing. If we are not resigned to death, our only way forward is to rise and join ranks with the cause of self-transformation—to get our severed, stiffened bodies up and moving again, radiating again, back on the road of life's endless journeys in pursuit of the castle that has all along been a part of each one of us.

Kafka does not explicitly tell us what exactly his cause is, as is typically difficult for artists to do so. The artist cannot tell; he can only, through repetitive "speaking," enable his cause to, like the castle, "occasionally reveal its stature," thereby stirring the reader's intrinsic memory, empowering the reader to ram through the gates of their own hell, to play a role in the great drama of freedom, directed by that long-confined, now liberated spirit. Such is the work of Kafka, as well as the defining characteristic of all so-called pure literature and artwork. You must carry on with this contradictory performance to become a true reader.

March 3, 2024

BRUNELDA'S SONG: READING KAFKA'S *AMERIKA*

Who would have expected that within the body of a poet as slender as a bamboo shoot there would be concealed such an immense, ponderous, ferociously domineering and manic artistic spirit? Yet here is Brunelda, the perpetually provocative queen of the city's night skies.

Once a member of the prosaic world, Brunelda had undergone the agonizing process of sloughing off everyday life. For the average person, this process is unimaginable: it demands a heart hardened even against kin and the courage to hold the existing state of affairs in contempt, to risk everything to forge one's own path. The proud Brunelda first drove away the husband who loved her so, turning him into a laughing stock, leaving him to wallow in despair. This was the queen's first step in her emancipation. What was she after? Her innermost desires drove her to the brink of insanity. What she wanted was an entirely new way of life, the establishment of her own artistic domain—that was what she wanted to do.

Though her entire body would billow with heat, and her great, fiery flesh could not be contained by her clothing, she nevertheless struggled to carry out her ambitions. She could not get by without the help of others, and her vitality, growing greater by the day, became ever more of a burden.

Then came a very special occasion. On that day, the huntress had been downstairs when her eyes alighted upon Delamarche, the vagabond, acknowledging him immediately, as he did her. She brought him all the way up to her dark abode at the top of a tall building. There, they fused into a unit, along with the other vagabond, Robinson.

And so, an emancipated Brunelda launched her true artistic career from the heights of her lofty abode. What is art? What is it, indeed? Art is torment, an inexhaustible, imaginative havoc, a relentless, repetitive plodding. What the wandering spirits of Delamarche and Robinson came to know in those extraordinary days was Brundelda's voluptuous flesh, brimming with vitality and contradiction. They understood immediately that only this woman could be their home, that only she could make it possible for them to realize their humanity, that it was she who would put an end to their incessant wandering so that they could begin creating in earnest. And yet dealing with such a volcanic body as Brunelda's was no easy task. From any given moment it was impossible to predict the next, and none of their efforts achieved the expected results. Day after day, in that dark, lofty temple of art, the threefold being of the two vagabonds and Queen Brunelda pursued their artistic project through trepidation and hope.

What an unbearable life it was! Tormented by her internal desires, the Queen appeared eccentric and unreasonable, vicious, demanding: she desired everything, and nothing less. Within a sealed, hidden chamber, her desire lay exposed, demanding no reply, rather a restrained obedience. And how could they not obey? Had the two wandering spirits not traveled there precisely for this purpose? Innately versed in the essence of art, Delamarche and Robinson understood how to stay vigilant, how to continually overcome their inertness to heed the queen's breath, drawing upon every bit of their powers of imagination to fulfill their communion with Brunelda. These vagabonds were skilled masters: through roundabout means, they expressed their humanity while simultaneously suppressing it.

It was Brunelda's flesh, an

insurmountable obstacle, that formed the foundation of the itinerants' predicament. In their eyes, she was an extraordinarily seductive beauty, yet frigid, an aloof goddess. For all his sexual engagement with Brunelda, Delamarche was entirely unable to experience the jubilation of her body, being left only with a bottomless yearning, a hunger born of lack. Whoever came to love Brunelda would suffer a lifetime of hunger. The hard labor of the flesh was never-ending, precluding any possibility of relief; yet, when forced into a dark corner, one begins to dream of the light. Sleeping out on the grimy balcony, breathing the polluted air, Robinson dreamt an intoxicating dream. In his dream, enveloped in the queen's enticing scent, he forgot his trauma and pain, to the point of self-abandon.

One could view this dreamland fantasy as compensation for the torments of his waking life, but it only aggravated his hunger. Vagabonds have no home; their homes are in their dreams, and Brunelda is precisely the source of those magnificent visions. This half-beastly, half-divine singer with her haughty red dress, her thick scent, her shameless exposure and crushing rejection—who could resist such double-edged enticement? "Brunelda, Brunelda, you primeval beauty, from where do you hail, to where do you lead us?", the vagabond asks repeatedly, through tears, in his dream, carrying a corner of the queen's dress with the utmost devotion, pursing his lips. Yet he is awoken with a start, and inside the apartment, Brunelda flies into a rage, cursing up a storm, knocking food onto the ground. Ultimately, Robinson remembers his obligations as a servant, pushes his sickly body up from the ground, and trudges inside for another day of hard labor.

In Brunelda converge manifold contradictions: she is a riddle that would stymie the average person. She is simultaneously coarse, heavy, and powerful, yet delicate, sensitive, and elegant.

Raging, she roars like a lion, yet she cannot bear the slightest disturbance. To her men, she is fervid, yet cold; she is infatuated with watching the masses downstairs, yet she lives a life of intense isolation from the outer world; she lives as a pristine artistic concept, yet her surroundings are unhygienic, unkempt and filthy; all day long she lies on a sofa bemoaning her sickness—yet in reality she possesses a stomach strong enough to digest spoiled food, and a robust heart that can withstand any sudden shock. Approaching Brunelda as such, if one wishes to fulfill her needs, what else is there to do but sink into a lifetime of servitude?

The two vagabonds, won over by her fantastical power, were perfectly willing to resign themselves to a life of hard labor. The young Karl's understanding of the queen is a slowly deepening one, evolving from mistrust, resentment and attempted rebellion to gradual comprehension, tolerance and, finally, collusion.

Karl's personal growth, as his own actor, proceeds along this course, owing to lessons nurtured from various environments. Of course, its primary contributor is still the queen's power. Whoever approaches her will experience a profoundly frightening sort of strength, because her will cannot be denied. This depiction of a hellish existence is a genuine portrait of the temple of art. Driven by fate, it is here that Karl will learn how to become an artist.

Towering over the city, is Brunelda's temple heaven or hell? Properly speaking, it resides somewhere in between. Just as Brunelda's own being is half-beast, half-goddess, the temple is an unparalleled amalgamation. It is a place that prohibits worldly intrusions, ethereal like no other, yet possesses all the traits of that exterior world, a site that lays bare humanity's yearning.

With her powerful physique,

Brunelda gathers extreme contradictions into a single being, as a fantastic space that, upon first impression, necessarily instills in us unfamiliarity and aversion. The charm of Brunelda's body is the charm of art itself, which moves one to yearn and dream, but refuses to provide even a sliver of satisfaction, and instead stokes the flames of yearning to burn ever brighter. In this temple, stripped of all else, the only thing one can do is dream, a beautiful kind of dreaming—amid torment, thirst and hunger. Those who do not believe in dreams will never be chosen by Brunelda. But how do the three who are chosen position themselves in this unique laboratory? What is the nature of their frenetic activity? As it turns out, their task is to dissolve boundaries, to enable two extremes to meet, two worlds to become one. This formidable labor is replete with pain and suffering, nightmares and hindrances, as well as hopeless struggle. And yet, now and again one hears a call from paradise. It is art, and only art, that realizes this kind of glorious consummation.

With a superhuman boldness of vision, Brunelda constructs this laboratory driven by the force of internal contradiction. She cannot be in paradise, as her infatuation with the mortal world is etched in her marrow; she cannot become enmeshed with those of the mundane world, as those interactions drive her mad. At this impasse, she can only turn to creation, and creating art, as a way out for her spirit.

The rise of Brunelda seems unfathomable. Yet one thing is for certain: she was born from an eruption of extreme repression, which has produced in her an unbridled callousness. In this eruption, she breaks out of confinement, casting aside her old life, establishing her own little domain out of thin air and becoming worthy of her queenly title.

Because this eruption was one of despair, all of her subsequent actions can only be the creation of something where there was previously nothing. In other words, she can only yield to her own volcanic flesh, so that her creativity, carried out with the help of the vagabonds, continues onward, for only then can she exist as herself.

April 8, 1998

THE RETURN OF GLORY: READING KAFKA'S "JOSEPHINE THE SONGSTRESS OR THE MOUSE FOLK"

Josephine—inspiration.
Us (the audience, opposition, little girls, etc.)—reason.
Music—ultimate beauty, eternal or desired.
Josephine's whistling—expressing music as the sound of the

mundane world (conscious). Our whistling—not expressing music as the sound of the mundane world (unconscious). Creative process—The conflicts and interdependence, breakthroughs, and mutual inclusion between Josephine and us.

Josephine and Us

Josephine is a miracle among us, our only window into eternal music. Music has long since disappeared from our realm of mundane existence; we have become accustomed to lives of hardship, to a world without music, with only casual whistling. Day in day out, our deteriorating bodies endure suffering. Then one day, Josephine suddenly appeared among us with her wondrous singing—a kind of irreplicable whistling.

This kind of singing that is not quite music seemed both foreign and familiar to us: it called to mind hymns of paradise we had never heard, yet it was also the very same whistling we heard every day. We know this isn't music, yet, without exception, each of us is deeply enthralled by it; its influence on us eclipses everything else in this mundane world. What connects us to Josephine's singing is a mysterious kind of feeling: indescribable, yet broadly felt.

All it takes is to sit across from this singer, watching her expressions as she sings, and we will be overcome with emotion. There is barely any difference between her whistling and ours; what moves us is her attitude toward singing, her condition while she sings. Who else can do it like her—who else can treat a performance of ordinary whistling as that of angel song? Only Josephine. While we are somewhat bewildered as to how she manages to sound forever novel to us, we feel that Josephine has provided us with an opportunity: through her whistling, our mind and body rise toward paradise. She instills in us a deep veneration, and that is enough.

In a world without music, we have learned to have faith in music; in a world without miracles, we come to believe in miracles. This may seem peculiar, and no one is able to explain it;

more likely, it's a kind of inheritance. Josephine is an embodiment of music and miracles. We adore Josephine, yet cannot fathom her singing, because her singing is unfathomable, so distant from what we expect music to sound like. But when we sit watching her whistle her tunes, our feelings are stirred. These feelings are ineffable: coloring the music are the hardships of our daily lives, all mixed together, indistinguishably. Listening attentively to Josephine we fall silent, and in the silence, we savor that long-awaited, paradisiacal peace.

It's true that these kinds of feelings are not equivalent to understanding. And yet, immersed in them, we congregate beside her to hear her whistle; this becomes our life's purpose, and the basis of her immense influence. So, we need Josephine, we cannot part with her for even a day—she is the one who creates in us a connection to music.

But do not assume that we idolize Josephine as perfection itself. We perceive Josephine as a whole: with her fickle and volatile child's temperament, her delicacy and vulnerability to injury, her aloofness toward the masses that borders on arrogance, and the total loneliness in her heart; we even know that she essentially holds us in contempt. For these reasons, our attitude toward her is to see her as a delicate child. We always strive to satisfy her demands, while at the same time, wishing to protect her as parents would a child. And given that she is a child under our protection, we naturally refrain from mocking any of her weaknesses. But that does not mean we do not see these weaknesses; we see them clearly, and so when we interact with her, we employ our quick wit skillfully, out of consideration for her.

If we are puzzled over her performances, the whistling that is neither aligned with our expectations of music, nor distinguishable from the sound of our own daily whistling, we keep our misgivings to ourselves. We resolve our internal contradiction by listening attentively to her, face-to-face. Furthermore, we are aware of her contempt for us, and know that our admiration for her does not move her, because what she seeks is an admiration of a specific sort, an absurd sort, a sort we are incapable of providing.

We also know that she uses our hindrances to her career, if not our complete lack of understanding of her, as an impetus to sing even more determinedly. That is, the more we get in the way of her goals, and the more we do not understand, the higher she holds her head. Knowing all this, we nevertheless adore her, and tune in with enthusiasm. Of course, when it is clear that her whistling is not music, we do experience a tiny bout of resistance (so as not to spoil her), but this does nothing to dispel our admiration for her. In the end, regarding ourselves as her parents, we do not expect to understand, but only appreciate. And how does Josephine feel about all of this?

Josephine's Suffering

Josephine's suffering stems from the ambiguous nature of her performances, which are entirely grounded in mundane life, yet conjure thoughts of paradise. Ever the dreamer, Josephine hails from the mundane world, a world she casts aside in her singing. She wants us to perceive her whistling as the sound of paradise, and to achieve this goal, she must suffer our lukewarm responses throughout her brief vocal career. She is plainly aware that we cannot accept her fantasies, yet her cause is precisely to realize that which cannot be. For this cause (or eccentric pastime), she empties her mind of all else, employing various tricks, concocting one method after another of self-torment, expending all her energies.

As humble people of the land, we admire Josephine, and have

continuously sought to help her. With our honest judgment and dogged faithfulness, not to mention astonishing patience, we enable Josephine's vocal performances to proceed smoothly time and time again. However, our attitude only adds to her suffering and aggravates the conflict in her heart.

This innately unusual woman is concerned with one matter only—an absurd, impossible matter, which is our validation of her art as supreme. This kind of delusion is built to fail. As we see it, Josephine's whistling is indeed charming and moves us to recollect the entirety of our experiences in this desolate world (lonely childhoods, premature aging in our prime and the loss of our ability to directly feel the music). Her whistling travels like news from humanity to each of our ears, reflecting the unstable existence of the individual within the collective, and upon listening to her, the tumult in our hearts settles temporarily once more.

But still—we cannot lie or speak deceptively. We can only say honestly that the sound of this whistling simply cannot be equated to the music of paradise; it bears too clearly the markings of mundanity. Josephine perceives our attitude as an attempt to stifle her, which only feeds her contempt and defiance toward us;

she vows to sway us with even higher standards of performance, going so far as to throw in some vulgar or banal gestures. Knowing it's no use, she continues; she has already been possessed.

Amid this showdown in the dark between suppression and resistance to suppression, Josephine suffers from exceptional self-torment, banking on sympathy softening our stance toward her demands. She has even forgotten that we are a people of principle, incapable of falsehood; no matter what tricks she employs, our stance will never waver. We have never seen paradise, yet we believe in it; Josephine's singing moves us to continually recall the legends, but that is all it does—it could never take the place of paradise itself. Did she not grow up among us, or does she claim to have fallen from the sky? No matter how Josephine tries, she can never shake off the signs of the mundane world. Her songs are storied with the lives of common folk.

On the other hand, it would be erroneous to think that Josephine solely scorns us, that she solely seeks to oppose us. She performs for us, and we are her only audience. As such, she also relies on us and draws from us the strength to sing; it's just that her manner of relying on us takes on a unique form. During her concerts, our existence, our small and large blows to her career, including our lack of understanding, the burdens of our soul—all become her stimulants, fomenting her determination to sing ever higher notes, so that we might be filled with profound veneration for her. When the passion of inspiration surges, such hindrances unexpectedly become necessary points of reference, because Josephine can then engage in "diametrically opposed action."

Environmental noise, and even the audience's dull gaze, together precondition the very act of Josephine's performing.

Yet, we were ultimately unable to fulfill Josephine's final wish, that is, her wish for us to validate her artistic genius. After unrelenting efforts, she finally fainted, achieving only a deep sense of dejection. And so, she disappeared. But disappearing does not mean giving up; absence further emphasizes prior existence. Our silent "people's memory" of her is as vivid as her actual performance. On this level, perhaps there is no difference whether an artist performs or not. For Josephine there is only process, without ultimate acknowledgement—that is her lamentable fate.

In fact, Josephine, ever loyal to singing, has never miscalculated, has never erred; that is to say, her very existence is predicated on "misunderstanding", being born in the mundane world, yet able to experience paradise. Quarreling with our folk over this kind of misunderstanding passed down from time immemorial, she whistles tune after tune of the mundane world with her hot-blooded youth, to express her yearning for paradise. And appear paradise does, precisely in the process of this artistic creation. But Josephine, positioned within the process, cannot see it. Perplexed as she is by the mundane nature of her performance and tormented by her inability to control the process (the process cannot be "controlled"), she can only continue singing. Our folk cannot see paradise either; we can only hear the whistling of the mundane world. Even as our imagination of paradise suffuses the air through the peculiar on- and off-again flow of her whistling, paradise itself remains immeasurably distant. We are able to clearly differentiate, and our levelheadedness and stubbornness are a fatal blow to Josephine. Pity we can only say with regret: she was too greedy.

If Josephine understood that paradise can only be realized through pursuits in the mundane world—i.e. that if you pursue it, it will appear, if you do not pursue it, it will not exist—would she still suffer so? It is likely, yes. Because it is only in the most painful moments that paradise genuinely appears, and she instinctively and impulsively calls to and grasps at these moments. In this respect, we could say that Josephine suffers a lifetime for momentary delight, and that her greatest delight is to exist within her greatest suffering. We could go one step further to say that Josephine's suffering itself is her effort to attain existence, that her suffering is a validation of life itself. And because the individual—likewise constituted by the people—is incapable of validating their own existence (when the object of reference is "absent"), this kind of suffering will extend on continuously, and so Josephine must continuously strive to "exist."

December 4, 1997

Can Xue is the pen name of the much lauded avant-garde writer Deng Xiaohua, who is the author of novels, short stories and works of criticism and philosophy that constitute an investigative literature of the soul. Her writing is characterized by the discerning eye of a reader, one in pursuit of poetic belonging. With an interplay between Chinese and western influences, and a distinct allegorical style, Can Xue's work has been a longtime favorite for the Nobel Prize in Literature.

Deanna Ren is a writer and translator working with an emphasis on decolonial translation theory and world literature. Interested in connections between music, art, history and everyday life, she regularly translates authors like Lu Xun and Can Xue. Ren graduated from Washington University in St. Louis with an MA in East Asian languages and cultures.

On Design (Series III)

The design for each book in Hanuman Editions Series III evokes *Thought-Forms: A Clairvoyant Investigation*, published by the revolutionary figure Annie Besant in 1905. Each book cover pays homage to a drawing from *Thought-Forms* and its rich imaginary of psychic abstraction that, like Hanuman Editions, has its roots in India, and travels recursively between disciplinary currents.

Our cover for *Kafka & I* conjures Besant's rendering of Wagner's music as a mountainous vibrational force, like the veiled castle with which the book begins. Among Can Xue's texts is a study of Kafka's 'Josephine the Songstress', a story of musical resonances foregrounded in the cover's harmonic melding of pinks and greens.

About the Press

Hanuman Editions is an independent publisher dedicated to avant-garde literature with an emphasis on translation. It reimagines the deconstructive legacy of Hanuman Books, the cult series published between Kalakshetra Press in southern India and the Chelsea Hotel in New York City from 1986 to 1993.

The press publishes individual volumes and limited edition box sets of contemporary works and select reissues from the Hanuman Books catalogue, as a polyphonic register of fiction, poetry, art and visual culture. Pithy and tactile, designed to slip in a pocket or the palm of a hand, the books serve as portals to a new and globally situated vanguard.

Kafka & I
Can Xue
translated by Deanna Ren

Published by
Hanuman Editions
London & Seattle
hanumaneditions.com

Founding Editor: Shruti Belliappa
Co-Editor: Joshua Rothes
Editorial Assistant: Moselle Kleiner

Publishers: Shruti Belliappa, Joshua Rothes
Design: Shruti Belliappa, Joshua Rothes
Typesetting: Joshua Rothes

Text © 2025 Can Xue
Translation 2025 Deanna Ren
Cover photo © Xiao Quan

First Edition. First printing.

ISBN 979-8-9893780-7-4

Printed in the UK on Fedrigoni Arena Natural.

Typeset in Arnhem Fine, with Eksell and Caslon No540 Swash D.

All rights reserved.

All rights reserved. No portion of this book may be reproduced in any form without written permission from the publisher or author, except as permitted by U.S. copyright law.

Like annals of a literary relationship, *Kafka & I* collects Can Xue's reflections on scenes of creation and destruction in Kafka's work, where women serve as agents of yearning or "prime movers" of art, roles refracted through the writer herself.